Holiday Hilarity: Christmas Jokes to Jingle Your Jolly

Dedicated to Katherine and Will

My gifts all year long

Holiday Hilarity: Christmas Jokes to Jingle Your Jolly   Nancy King

Holiday Hilarity

Christmas Jokes to Jingle Your Jolly

Nancy King

Holiday Hilarity: Christmas Jokes to Jingle Your Jolly — Nancy King

What does Santa say after too many midnight treats?

"OH, OH, OH, I don't feel so good."

Holiday Hilarity: Christmas Jokes to Jingle Your Jolly   Nancy King

What holiday message does the cow share?

"Have a very moo-ry Christmas!"

Holiday Hilarity: Christmas Jokes to Jingle Your Jolly — Nancy King

How does the chef approach the Christmas season?

As the perfect time to "whisk" you a Merry Christmas!

Holiday Hilarity: Christmas Jokes to Jingle Your Jolly   Nancy King

How do elves get to the top of Santa's workshop?

They use the "elf"evator!

Holiday Hilarity: Christmas Jokes to Jingle Your Jolly — Nancy King

Why did Mrs. Johnson wear sunglasses to the Christmas party?

Because her students were so bright.

Holiday Hilarity: Christmas Jokes to Jingle Your Jolly   Nancy King

Why did the kitten love her Christmas gift?

The box was purr-fectly wrapped.

Holiday Hilarity: Christmas Jokes to Jingle Your Jolly		Nancy King

How much did Santa pay for his sleigh?

Nothing. It was on the house.

Holiday Hilarity: Christmas Jokes to Jingle Your JollyNancy King

What's the best thing to give your parents for Christmas?

A list of what you want!

Holiday Hilarity: Christmas Jokes to Jingle Your Jolly   Nancy King

Why did Santa have to go to the doctor?

He had tinsel-itis!

Holiday Hilarity: Christmas Jokes to Jingle Your Jolly   Nancy King

What do the reindeer do in their off hours?

They play s-table tennis.

Holiday Hilarity: Christmas Jokes to Jingle Your Jolly — Nancy King

What treat do twins enjoy most at Christmas time?

Double-baked cookies.

Holiday Hilarity: Christmas Jokes to Jingle Your Jolly Nancy King

How do sheep south of the border greet friends at Christmas?

Fleece Navidad.

Holiday Hilarity: Christmas Jokes to Jingle Your Jolly   Nancy King

What is the relationship of the elves to Santa Claus?

They are subordinate clauses.

Holiday Hilarity: Christmas Jokes to Jingle Your Jolly　　　　　　　　　　Nancy King

Why did Mrs. Claus open a bakery in the off-season?

She kneaded the dough.

Holiday Hilarity: Christmas Jokes to Jingle Your Jolly Nancy King

How did the gingerbread man walk when he broke his foot?

With a candy cane.

Holiday Hilarity: Christmas Jokes to Jingle Your Jolly — Nancy King

What do you call Santa when he takes a break on the job?

Santa Pause.

Holiday Hilarity: Christmas Jokes to Jingle Your Jolly   Nancy King

Why did the astronauts ignore the festive dinner table?

They'd already had a big launch.

Holiday Hilarity: Christmas Jokes to Jingle Your Jolly Nancy King

What holiday song does the veterinarian sing with the dogs?

"Bark the Herald Angels Sing."

Holiday Hilarity: Christmas Jokes to Jingle Your Jolly   Nancy King

Why did the little boy sleep under the car on Christmas Eve?

Because he wanted to wake up really oily.

Holiday Hilarity: Christmas Jokes to Jingle Your Jolly Nancy King

What do Santa's junior elves do after school?

Their gnome work.

Holiday Hilarity: Christmas Jokes to Jingle Your Jolly　　　Nancy King

Why did Rudolph cross the road?

He saw the 'Deer Crossing' sign.

Holiday Hilarity: Christmas Jokes to Jingle Your Jolly   Nancy King

What's Frosty's favorite Christmas song?

"Snow No Place Like Home for the Holidays."

Holiday Hilarity: Christmas Jokes to Jingle Your Jolly   Nancy King

Why was Santa's head elf so good at telling jokes?

He always delivered the punch line in the nick of time.

Holiday Hilarity: Christmas Jokes to Jingle Your Jolly Nancy King

Why did Santa keep going to the candy store?

He was stocking up.

Holiday Hilarity: Christmas Jokes to Jingle Your Jolly Nancy King

Why did the Elf on the Shelf bring a ladder to work?

Because he heard the job had its ups and downs!

Holiday Hilarity: Christmas Jokes to Jingle Your Jolly   Nancy King

What's Santa's music of choice for the workshop?

W-rap music.

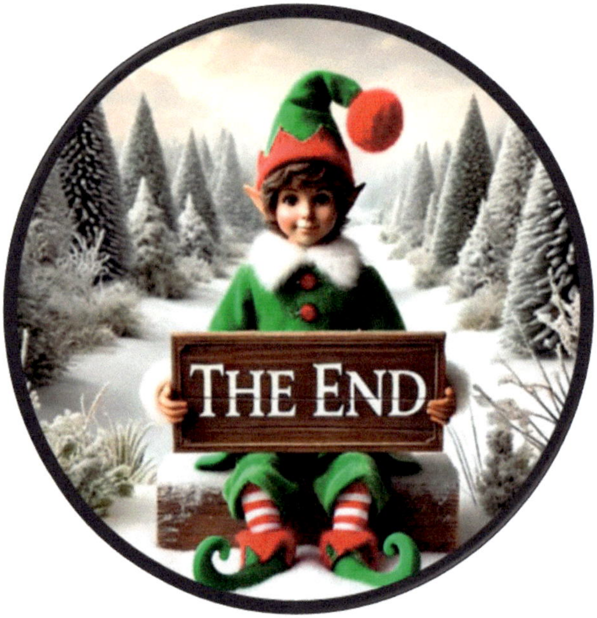
THE END

About the Author

Nancy King is a North Carolina poet, writer, filmmaker, and artist.

She has written, illustrated, and published over thirty books, many for children. Her writings include short stories, chapter books, poetry collections, and jokes as well as many audio stories; and lyrics for over 150 songs.

A member of the Writing, Music & Film Society, Nancy loves to collaborate with other writers and creative friends. Her feature film, 'Cora's Ring' premieres in 2024.

Books: amazon.com

Audio stories and more: anotheroneplease.etsy.com

Music: alanikeiser.com

Other books by Nancy King

Halloween Jokes
Udderly Hilarious: You Herd it Here First (collaborative)
Udderly Hilarious: Here We Goat Again (collaborative)
Awenasa and Yunwi Tsunsdi In the Great Smoky Mountains
Nocturnal Animals of the World
Honey, A Golden Gift of Life (rhyming)
Curious Bunny (rhyming)
Delores the Duck Who Wanted to Be A Ballerina
James Loves Noises (rhyming, personalized))
Welcome to the World (personalized)
COLORS Everywhere I Look
Whiskers and Violet: A Forever Friendship (rhyming)
ROMEO The Self-Doubting Hedgehog
My Favorite Color?
MAPACHE The Raccoon Who Thought He Was A Dog
Regina and the Great Migration
Cody The Dreamweaver Coyote
ANASTASIA Dreamkeeper to the Frogs

Holiday Hilarity: Christmas Jokes to Jingle Your Jolly   Nancy King

Heard Any Good Chicken Jokes Lately? (collaborative)
Heard Any Good Pirate Jokes Lately?
The Girl Who Loved Goats (beginning chapter book)
Sticks Are People Too
Beach Friends Forever
Which Witch Is Which? (rhyming)
Leave The Rest to Me (rhyming)
Jokes For Simon
Mrs. Melton's Flower Garden
The Fire Within (fourth grade spelling words)
My Words Shall Set Me Free (poetry)
The Words You Sent to Me (poetry)
My Words Have Wings (poetry)
Beginning Again (collaborative)
And Return In The Spring (collaborative)
As The Quay Turns (collaborative)

Plutocracy Publications, LLC
2024, All Rights Reserved
Images incorporate ai technology, modified as needed by Nancy King

Made in the USA
Columbia, SC
22 August 2024